Congressional
Research
Service

Monitoring and Verification in Arms Control

Amy F. Woolf
Specialist in Nuclear Weapons Policy

December 23, 2011

Congressional Research Service

7-5700

www.crs.gov

R41201

CRS Report for Congress
Prepared for Members and Committees of Congress

Summary

The United States and Russia signed a new START Treaty on April 8, 2010, and the treaty entered into force on February 5, 2011. Many analysts, both in the United States and Russia, supported negotiations on a new treaty so that the two sides could continue to implement parts of the complex monitoring and verification regime in the 1991 START Treaty. This regime was designed to build confidence in compliance with the START and to provide transparency and cooperation during the treaty's implementation. The verification regime in the new START Treaty differs in some respects from the regime in START. These differences reflect an interest in reducing the cost and complexity of the regime, updating it to account for changes in the relationship between the United States and Russia, and tailoring it to address the monitoring and verification complexities presented by the new limits in the new treaty. The verification regime received scrutiny in both the Senate, which voted on December 22, 2010, to consent to ratification, and the public.

Verification is the process that one country uses to assess whether another country is complying with an arms control agreement. To verify compliance, a country must determine whether the forces or activities of another country are within the bounds established by the limits and obligations in the agreement. A verifiable treaty contains an interlocking web of constraints and provisions designed to deter cheating, to make cheating more complicated and more expensive, or to make its detection more timely. In the past, the United States has deemed treaties to be effectively verifiable if it has confidence that it can detect militarily significant violations in time to respond and offset any threat that the violation may create for the United States.

The United States and Russia rely on their own national technical means of verification (NTM) to collect most of the information needed to verify compliance with arms control agreements. But, since the 1980s, the treaties have also mandated that the two sides share information through data exchanges and notifications, and conduct on-site inspections to confirm that information. The verification regime in START used these monitoring measures not only to confirm that forces were consistent with the limits in the treaty, but also to detect and deter potential efforts to violate the treaty. With the end of the Cold War and the new relationship with Russia, the United States and Russia may both have more confidence in the other side's intent to comply with its arms control obligations. However, both will still want to monitor the other's forces and activities to confirm compliance and to foster cooperation and transparency.

This report reviews some of the monitoring and verification provisions in the new START Treaty and compares these with some of the provisions in the original START Treaty. It focuses, specifically, on differences between the treaties in the provisions governing the exchange of data, known as telemetry, generated during missile flight tests; provisions governing the monitoring of mobile intercontinental ballistic missiles (ICBMs); and differences in the numbers and types of on-site inspections.

This report will be updated as needed.

Contents

Tables

Contacts

Introduction

The United States and Russia signed a new START Treaty, officially known as the *Treaty between the United States of America and the Russian Federation on Measures to Further Reduction and Limitation of Strategic Offensive Arms*, on April 8, 2010. This treaty is, in part, designed to replace the 1991 Strategic Offensive Reductions Treaty (START), which expired, after 15 years of implementation, on December 5, 2009. The Senate Foreign Relations Committee, Armed Services Committee, and Intelligence Committee all held hearings and briefings on the treaty. The Foreign Relations Committee approved a resolution of Ratification for the Treaty on September 16, 2010. The full Senate debated the treaty in mid-December 2010 and gave its advice and consent to ratification, by a vote of 71-26, on December 22, 2010. The Russian parliament approved the treaty on January 25 and 26, 2011. New START entered into force on February 5, 2011, after the United States and Russia exchanged the instruments of ratification.

During the latter years of the George W. Bush Administration, as the calendar moved closer to the expiration of START, the United States and Russia began to identify steps they might take to preserve parts of the START legacy while charting a new direction for arms control.[1] Throughout this time, Russia sought to replace START with a new treaty that would maintain the general structure of START, with limits on deployed warheads and delivery vehicles and detailed definitions and counting rules that would capture the full range of strategic capabilities within the treaty limits. The Bush Administration did not want to replace START with a formal treaty, but proposed that the parties replace START with a modified version of the 2002 Moscow Treaty,[2] counting only the declared number of deployed strategic warheads, and an annex that would permit the continuation of some of the monitoring and verification provisions in START.

There was widespread agreement, both within the U.S. policy community and between the United States and Russia, that there would be value in continuing some parts of the complex START monitoring and verification regime. The provisions were designed to build confidence in compliance with the specific limits and restrictions in the treaty, but they also provided a level of detail in information that contributed to each nation's general understanding of the other's forces and activities and helped build cooperation between them. Both nations wanted to modify the regime to ease some of its complexity, reduce the costs associated with its notifications and inspections, and minimize its interference with ongoing military operations. Both also recognized the value of continuing some level of transparency and cooperation.

Several Members of Congress also spoke in support of proposals to extend the monitoring and verification regime in START. For example, a mid-2007 "Dear Colleague" letter called for the core elements of the START verification regime to be extended, explaining that "the transparency required by the START verification regime has bred confidence in both Russia and the U.S., enabling cooperation on a range of nuclear arms control issues. Moreover, verification directly supports U.S. national security interests by giving insight into Russia's arsenal of nuclear weapons."[3] Senator Richard Lugar has also stated that "the current U.S.-Russian relationship is

---

[1] For a summary of this process, see CRS Report R40084, *Strategic Arms Control After START: Issues and Options*, by Amy F. Woolf.

[2] For details on this Treaty, see CRS Report RL31448, *Nuclear Arms Control: The Strategic Offensive Reductions Treaty*, by Amy F. Woolf.

[3] Call on the President to extend the most Significant Remaining Arms Control Agreement Of our Time. July, 2009.

complicated enough without introducing more elements of uncertainty. Failure to preserve the START Treaty would increase the potential for distrust between the two sides."[4] Similarly, Senator Jon Kyl expressed his support for START's verification regime, noting in November 2009 that, after START expires, "the U.S. will lose a significant source of information that has allowed it to have confidence in its ability to understand Russian strategic nuclear forces; likewise, the Russian Federation will lose information about the U.S. nuclear forces."[5]

The Obama Administration altered the U.S. approach toward arms control and the pending expiration of START. In April 2009, he and President Medvedev agreed that the United States and Russia would negotiate a formal agreement to replace START. In a joint statement released at their meeting, the Presidents indicated that the new treaty would not only reduce strategic offensive arms below the levels in the Moscow Treaty, but would also "include effective verification measures drawn from the experience of the Parties in implementing the START Treaty."[6] The negotiating teams from both parties included participants who had worked as inspectors under the original START Treaty; their experience and expertise helped the nations modify the monitoring and verification regime for the new START Treaty.

When the two sides completed the negotiations in March 2010, the Obama Administration noted that "the Treaty has a verification regime that combines the appropriate elements of the 1991 START Treaty with new elements tailored to the limitations of the Treaty." The Administration also indicated that "the inspections and other verification procedures in this Treaty will be simpler and less costly to implement than the old START treaty. In part, this is possible due to the experience and knowledge gained from 15 years of START implementation."[7] The regime will include "on-site inspections and exhibitions, data exchanges and notifications related to strategic offensive arms and facilities covered by the Treaty, and provisions to facilitate the use of national technical means for treaty monitoring." It would also mandate the exchange of some telemetry generated during missile flight tests.[8] Admiral Mullen emphasized during a press conference announcing the treaty's completion that the new treaty "features a much more effective, transparent verification method that demands quicker data exchanges and notifications" than did START.[9]

During its first 11 months in force, the United States and Russia have conducted over 1,700 exchanges of notifications and several exhibitions, as mandated by the treaty. The United States has conducted 16 inspections at Russian facilities, while Russia has conducted 17 inspections at U.S. facilities.[10] These inspections occurred at ICBM, SLBM, and heavy bomber bases, storage

---

[4] Senator Richard Lugar. "Trust Still Needs Verification." *Washington Times*. July 18, 2008. p. 24.

[5] Senator Jon Kyl, "NSWG Travel," Remarks in the Senate, *Congressional Record*, daily edition. November 21, 2009. p. S11969.

[6] The White House, Office of the Press Secretary, *Joint Statement ... Regarding Negotiations on Further Reductions in Strategic Offensive Arms* , Washington, D.C., April 1, 2009, http://www.whitehouse.gov/the_press_office/Joint-Statement-by-Dmitriy-A-Medvedev-and-Barack-Obama/.

[7] The White House, Office of the Press Secretary, *Readout of the President's call with Russian President Medvedev*, Washington, DC, March 25, 2010, http://www.whitehouse.gov/the-press-office/readout-presidents-call-with-russian-president-medvedev-0.

[8] The White House, Office of the Press Secretary, *Key Facts About the New START Treaty*, Washington, D.C., March 26, 2010, http://www.whitehouse.gov/the-press-office/key-facts-about-new-start-treaty.

[9] U.S. Department of State, *Announcement of the New START Treaty*, Washington, D.C., March 26, 2010, http://www.state.gov/secretary/rm/2010/03/139147 htm.

[10] Rose Gottemoeller, "A "New START" For Arms Control," *The Hill*, December 22, 2011. http://thehill.com/blogs/ (continued...)

---

facilities, conversion and elimination facilities, and test ranges. The parties have held two sessions of the Bilateral Consultative Commission (BCC), which was established by the treaty to address implementation and compliance issues.

Verification was one of the central concerns addressed in the Senate and in the public literature, during the debate over the substance and implications of the new START Treaty. Some questioned whether the monitoring provisions in the new treaty are sufficient to provide the United States with enough information to either confirm Russian compliance with the treaty or detect efforts to violate its terms; others questioned whether the provisions will provide Russia with too much access to and information about U.S. nuclear forces and activities. The cooperative monitoring measures in the treaty, and, particularly, the inspection process, received special scrutiny, as many observers of the arms control process specifically measured the value of the monitoring and verification regime by its widespread use of notifications, on-site inspections, and other cooperative measures. However, these measures are only a part of the elaborate process that allowed the United States and Russia to maintain confidence in each other's compliance with the original START Treaty. An evaluation of the monitoring and verification regime in the new treaty would, therefore, assess the full range of treaty terms, monitoring systems, and analysis tools that constitute a verification regime.

This report provides background information about the role that these terms and tools play in the verification process. It highlights, more generally, the way that monitoring and verification provisions interact with the limits and restrictions in a treaty to provide confidence in compliance. It does not evaluate whether the provisions in the new START Treaty are sufficient to judge that the treaty is "effectively verifiable," but, instead, identifies some of the differences between the verification provisions in START and new START, then describes how these changes derive from differences in the limits in the two treaties.

Monitoring and Verification in Arms Control

The Components of a Verification Regime

Verification is the process that one country uses to assess whether another country is complying with an arms control agreement. To verify compliance, a country must determine whether the forces or activities of another country are within the bounds established by the limits and obligations in the agreement. No treaty relies on any one provision as the basis for successful monitoring and verification. A verifiable treaty contains an interlocking web of constraints and provisions designed to deter cheating, to make cheating more complicated and more expensive, or to make its detection more timely. There are five key components in a verification regime: treaty language, monitoring, analysis, evaluation, and resolution.

Treaty language forms the core of the verification regime.[11] By describing the limits and obligations that parties must observe, it identifies the forces and activities that comply with the

---

(...continued)

congress-blog/foreign-policy/200997-a-new-start-for-arms-control.

[11] Richard A. Scribner, Theodore J. Ralston, and William D. Metz, *The Verification Challenge: Problems and Promise of Strategic Nuclear Arms Control Verification* (Boston: Birkhauser, 1985), pp. 24-25.

---

terms of the treaty. The identification of compliant activities helps a country focus on what it should look for when it monitors the other country's forces and activities. Treaty language also includes collateral constraints that might help a country determine whether the other country's forces and activities are compatible with the limits and obligations. Collateral constraints might include

- restrictions, such as a ban on activities that might interfere with the collection of information about restricted forces and activities;

- obligations, such as the requirement that all restricted forces be located in specified facilities and areas; and

- cooperative measures, such as the exchange of data about the forces that are limited by the treaty.

Monitoring systems collect data on the forces and activities of another country. The United States and Russia use several monitoring systems, usually referred to as the national technical means of verification (NTM), that operate outside the territory of the other country. These include photoreconnaisance satellites, radar installations, and electronic surveillance capabilities.[12] The United States and Russia would use these systems even if they did not have to verify compliance with arms control agreements because they provide basic intelligence information about the other country's forces and activities.

The United States and Russia also operate monitoring systems, usually referred to as on-site inspections, inside the other country's territory. These include visits by inspection teams, manned observation posts outside selected facilities, and sensors at specific locations to monitor activities occurring nearby. While each nation would operate NTM whether or not they were a party to an arms control regime, the on-site inspections and other cooperative monitoring mechanisms only operate within the framework established by a treaty's verification regime.

The types of data and information needed to verify compliance with arms control obligations may not be the same as the information sought for intelligence purposes.[13] The information collected through the intelligence process may include data on weapons characteristics or military operations that are not limited by the treaty. This information may be useful in assessing the capabilities of an adversary's forces, but it may not be needed to determine whether those forces are consistent with the obligations in a treaty.

Hence, the information needed to verify compliance with a treaty may be more discrete and specific than the general information desired for intelligence purposes. Moreover, a monitoring regime designed to aid with the verification of compliance with one agreement may not be either useful or necessary in the verification of compliance with another agreement. The verification regime would have been tailored to provide the information needed to verify compliance with the specific limits in the treaty. Consequently, when assessing the value of a treaty's verification regime, it is important not only to distinguish between the intelligence value and the verification

---

[12] For descriptions of the systems included in the National Technical Means of Verification, see Scribner, Ralston, and Metz, The Verification Challenge, pp. 47-66. See also Ted Greenwood. *Reconnaissance, Surveillance, and Arms Control.* Adelphi Paper #88, London, International Institute for Strategic Studies, 1972; and John Pike. *Eyes in the Sky: Satellite Reconnaissance.* International Review. August/September 1988. pp. 21-26.

[13] William Colby. *The Intelligence Process.* In Kosta Tsipis, David W. Hafemeister, and Penny Janeway, ed. *Arms Control Verification: The Technologies That Make it Possible.* (Washington, Pergamon-Brassey's, 1986), p. 11.

value of information collected by the monitoring systems, but also to recognize the relationship between the limits and restrictions in a treaty and the scope of the monitoring provisions.

The *analysis process* refines the data collected by the monitoring systems to help develop a picture of the other country's forces and activities. The United States and Russia collect a vast amount of information about each other with their NTM. The images and transmissions provided by the NTM must be sorted and interpreted before a country can determine whether they reveal forces and activities that comply with the terms of an arms control treaty. The analysts evaluate information to determine whether it is relevant and reliable, they compare information from different sources to resolve ambiguities in the data, and they combine information from different sources to develop a broader picture of the other country's activities.[14]

Although the analysis process translates data collected by the monitoring systems into more usable information, it may not determine the precise meaning of the information. In some cases, the collection of additional information could reduce uncertainties by helping to resolve ambiguities or by fleshing out existing data. Additional data might also complicate the analysis process if it were unreliable or inconsistent with existing information. Consequently, the picture presented by the analysis process will necessarily display some unclear and uncertain results.

The *evaluation* portion of the verification regime determines whether the other country has complied with the terms of the arms control treaty. It is essentially a political, rather than technical, process that assesses whether the information collected by the monitoring systems and refined by the analysis process reveals forces and activities that satisfy the limits and obligations defined by the treaty language.[15] The answers will not always be obvious. In some cases, the treaty language may not clearly identify the activities that comply with or violate the treaty. In addition, the information about the other country's activities will almost certainly contain some uncertainties that could not be resolved in the analysis process. This indicates that verification is almost always a matter of judgment. Political leaders must decide whether the information provides evidence of compliance or violation. They must determine whether ambiguous activities are significant and whether those activities might create unacceptable risks for their own country.

The *resolution* phase of the verification regime occurs if the participants in the evaluation process conclude that the forces and activities of the other country do not satisfy the limits and obligations in the treaty. The country reaching that conclusion must decide how to respond to the evidence of a possible violation. The country discovering the violation could raise its concerns with the other country, so that it could either convince the other country to correct the violation or provide the other country with an opportunity to explain its activities. This dialogue could take place through normal diplomatic channels, or it could occur in a forum that the treaty had established for the discussion and resolution of compliance questions.[16] If the violation continues, a country could respond with changes in its own forces to register its objection to the violation, and, if the violation creates a new threat to the country's security, to offset any benefits that the other country might have gained with the violation. In the extreme, the country that discovered the violation might abrogate the treaty, so that it would not be bound by any of the limits, and deploy the forces

---

[14] Noel Gaylorl. *Verification, Compliance, and the Intelligence Process.* In Tsipis, Hafemeister, and Janeway, ed. Arms Control Verification. pp. 5-6.

[15] U.S. Arms Control and Disarmament Agency. *Verification, The Critical Element of Arms Control.* Publication 85. March 1976. Washington, 1976. p. 5.

[16] The New START Treaty will create a Bilateral Consultative Commission for this purpose.

that it believes are needed to restore its security. In any case, the response that a country chooses to resolve its concerns will probably reflect the nature of the violation and the threat it might pose to that country's security.

The Objectives of a Verification Regime

The verification regime in an arms control treaty cannot remove all doubts about the existence of possible violations. Nonetheless, it may provide each country with confidence in the other's compliance with the treaty if it accomplishes three distinct objectives. First, the regime should permit the countries to detect evidence that violations might have occurred. The data collected by the monitoring systems, when combined with the restrictions in the treaty, should enable each country to identify violations that could create a significant threat to its security in a timely fashion.[17]

Second, the verification regime should deter violations to the treaty. It might accomplish this objective if the country considering an activity that would violate the agreement believed that the benefits it might gain with the activity were overshadowed by the possible costs, including the financial expense and the possible consequences if the activity were detected.[18] By collecting a wide range of information on forces and activities, the verification regime increases the likelihood that significant violations will be detected. If the country considering the violation found this risk unacceptable, and the possible consequences if the violation were discovered, it might try to conceal its activities. However, the need to construct new facilities or alter existing facilities to conceal noncompliant forces or activities would add to the cost of the violation and could possibly reduce the country's confidence in the military value of the systems involved in the violation. This would possibly discourage the violation.

Third, the verification regime should help build confidence in the viability of the arms control treaty. Evidence that the countries are complying with limits and obligations in the treaty is a key source of confidence in the agreement. The verification regime can also build confidence if it provides each country with a better understanding of the other country's forces and activities and if it demonstrates that the countries are committed to the arms control process. Although these contributions may be more difficult to measure than evidence of compliance, they can be as important in efforts to build and maintain support for arms control.

This last element of the verification process proved to be particularly valuable during the implementation of the START Treaty. Fifteen years of experience demonstrated that the United States and Russia could work together to monitor forces and activities and to resolve compliance questions, while gaining a better understanding of the forces and activities of the other nation. The two governments have had to communicate and cooperate to resolve questions about the military forces that are central to their national security goals. Many analysts highlighted this benefit of the START verification regime as the primary reason why the two nations should continue the monitoring process. Some have argued that the new START Treaty will also prove to

---

[17] U.S. Arms Control and Disarmament Agency. Verification: The Critical Element of Arms Control. pp. 1-2. See also U.S. Arms Control and Disarmament Agency. Annual Report to Congress, 1988. Washington, 1989. p. 55.

[18] Sidney N. Graybeal and Patricia Bliss McFate. *Criteria For Verification: In the Eyes of the Beholder?* International Review. August/September 1988. pp. 5-6.

be valuable, regardless of its specific limits on deployed forces, if it continues the tradition of transparency and cooperation.[19]

Assessing Verifiability

No treaty is "100% verifiable"; each carries some risk that some noncompliant activities may go unnoticed, either entirely or until they become problems for either the viability of the treaty regime or the security of the treaty participants. In crafting and assessing a treaty, analysts try to convey the degree of risk that "militarily significant violations"—those that might undermine the security of the treaty participants—would go undetected.

During the 1970s, when the United States and Soviet Union were participating in the Strategic Arms Limitation (SALT) talks, the United States assessed a treaty to be "adequately verifiable" if it had high confidence that it could detect evidence of militarily significant violations in time to respond to the violations and offset any potential security risk they might create. During the 1980s, when the United States and Soviet Union were negotiating the Intermediate-Range Nuclear Forces (INF) Treaty and the Strategic Arms Reduction Treaty (START), officials in the Reagan Administration argued that the standard of "adequate verification" was inadequate. They believed the Soviet Union had demonstrated that it might violate some provisions in treaties even if the violations created no military risk for the United States, and they argued that the United States should be able to detect and respond to these types of violations. Even if they created no military risk, the United States might still bear a political cost if the Soviet Union were seen as violating arms control treaties at will. Therefore, it identified a new standard of "effective verification" for arms control treaties. This standard essentially meant that the United States should be able to detect not only militarily significant violations in time to respond and counter any potential threat, but also other types of violations or discrepancies where it might need to employ a political response.

In practice, however, particularly when testifying in support of a treaty's ratification, the two standards seemed to be quite similar. For example, when testifying in support of the INF Treaty in 1988, Paul Nitze, who had served as an arms control advisor and negotiator in the Reagan Administration, stated that "I am confident that, in the INF agreement we have succeeded in working out measures which give one high confidence, not perfect confidence, but high confidence that it would be impossible for them to deploy a militarily meaningful military component for any period of time without our having the very real prospect that we would be able to get some indication thereof."[20] Moreover, Ambassador Nitze noted that this conclusion was due not only to the monitoring and inspection regime in the treaty, but also to the clarity of the treaty text and the associated restrictions on forces and facilities.

To a great extent, the job of assessing the verifiability of an arms control agreement rests with the intelligence community. And central to this assessment is an evaluation of the ways in which a treaty partner may seek to evade or exceed the limits in the treaty. Both the opportunities and motivations for treaty violations depend, in part, on the terms of the treaty. But assessing the likelihood that a party would pursue a particular cheating scenario is also an analytic exercise that

---

[19] Pavel Podvig, "Assessing START Follow-on," *Bulletin of the Atomic Scientists On-line*, March 29, 2010. http://russianforces.org/blog/2010/03/assessing_start_follow-on.shtml.

[20] U.S. Congress, Senate Foreign Relations, *The INF Treaty*, Hearing, 100th Cong., 2nd sess., February 1, 2008, S. Hrg. 100-522 pr. 2 (Washington: GPO, 1988), pp. 80-81.

---

may reflect the political climate of the time. One can either begin with the assumption that a party to the treaty would want to retain excess forces or engage in activities limited by the treaty so that could retain or acquire additional military capabilities and advantages. In contrast, one might also begin with the assumption that both parties to the treaty are committed to implementing the limits and restrictions in the treaty, and that neither would knowingly or intentionally try to exceed the limits for military or political gain.

Many in the United States believed that the Soviet Union would take the first approach during the 1970s and 1980s. Some in the United States, therefore, imagined elaborate scenarios that defined how the Soviet Union might develop, deploy, and retain missiles and warheads in excess of treaty limits. The monitoring provisions sought for both the INF and START Treaties were then designed to provide information that would reveal efforts to implement these potential cheating scenarios.

The changing political and security environments in the 1990s and 2000s, and the improving relationship between the United States and Russia, altered the assumptions about Russian incentives for noncompliance and, therefore, eased concerns about cheating scenarios. Secretary of Defense Rumsfeld made this point in his testimony before the Senate Foreign Relations Committee on the 2002 Moscow Treaty. He stated that the Bush Administration "saw no need to include detailed verification measures in the treaty" because "neither side has an interest in evading the terms of the treaty since it simply codifies unilateral announced intentions and reductions."[21]

The assessment of a treaty's verifiability is not a statement of whether the United States can or would respond to a particular violation if it were to occur. The decision of whether and how to respond would depend, in part, on whether the United States had the capability to respond. This determination was essentially at the core of the assessments of treaty verifiability in the 1970s and 1980s. Many analysts believed that, even if the United States did detect Soviet violations, it would not respond because it would either lack the military capability or the political will to do so. This led many to argue, that no matter how closely the United States monitored Soviet forces and activities, the treaties were not in the U.S. national security interest because the Soviet Union would violate them and the United States would not respond.

The decision of whether and how to respond to treaty violations would also reflect an assessment of whether, and how, the violation might undermine U.S. security. During the Cold War, it was often assumed that any violation that allowed the Soviet Union to gain a military, or even political, edge over the United States would undermine U.S. security. But this assessment changed when the Bush Administration indicated that it was not concerned about the military implications of potential Russian violations to the 2002 Strategic Offensive Reductions Treaty. Secretary Rumsfeld pointed out that the United States no longer sized or structured its military forces as a response to the Russian threat, and it planned to reduce its weapons with or without a treaty and with or without Russian reductions.[22] As a result, even if Russia violated the treaty and did not reduce its forces, the United States would have no reason to respond with force increases of its own.

---

[21] U.S. Congress, Senate Foreign Relations, *Treaty on Strategic Offensive Reductions: The Moscow Treaty*, Hearing, 107th Cong., 2nd sess., July 17, 2002, S. Hrg. 107-622 (Washington: GPO, 2002), p. 79.

[22] U.S. Congress, Senate Foreign Relations, *Treaty on Strategic Offensive Reductions: The Moscow Treaty*, Hearing, 107th Cong., 2nd sess., July 17, 2002, S. Hrg. 107-622 (Washington: GPO, 2002), p. 79.

Monitoring and Verification in U.S.-Soviet and U.S.-Russian Arms Control[23]

The United States and Soviet Union began to include verification provisions in arms control agreements signed as early as the late 1950s. For the most part, the parties to these treaties planned to rely on NTM to monitor the forces and activities of other participating states. Moreover, the arms control process benefited, and agreements became more common, because these technologies developed to the point where the parties could use them to gather the information they needed to develop confidence in compliance and detect violations.

Many of the agreements signed in the 1950s and 1960s also called for some level of cooperation between the parties in monitoring compliance. They did not, however, provide the participating nations with access to either U.S. or Soviet territory, or information about U.S. and Soviet military activities. For example, the Antarctic Treaty, signed in 1959, permitted on-site inspections at facilities on Antarctica. But because the treaty permitted only peaceful, scientific installations on Antarctica, these inspections would not provide any information about military forces or activities unless they existed in violation of the treaty. Similarly, the Outer Space Treaty, signed in 1967, permitted on-site inspections to confirm the absence of weapons of mass destruction at installations on the moon or other celestial bodies. Even the 1964 Limited Test Ban Treaty, which was made possible by the ability of NTM to monitor the location of nuclear explosions, lacked any provision authorizing the collection of information about military activities. Moreover, the treaty did not extend to a prohibition on underground tests, in part, because the United States and Soviet Union could not agree on the number of on-site inspections they would need to monitor compliance with that type of provision.

The bilateral arms control agreements between the United States and Soviet Union during the 1970s relied on a similar formula. For the most part, the two nations recognized that each would use its own NTM to collect the information needed to confirm compliance and detect violations. At the same time, the treaties included some cooperative measures that were designed to help NTM gain access to the necessary information. For example, in the 1972 Anti-ballistic Missile Treaty and Interim Agreement on Offensive Arms—the agreements signed as a part of the Strategic Arms Limitation Talks (SALT)—the United States and Soviet Union acknowledged that they would use NTM to monitor systems limited by the treaties. They also agreed that they would not interfere with the other country's NTM or conceal their forces or activities in ways that would impede verification by NTM. They did not, however, specify what types of activities might impede NTM.

In the SALT II Treaty, signed in 1979, the countries expanded their pledge not to interfere with the collection of information. Because the treaty restricted changes in weapons characteristics, as well as weapon numbers, it banned the deliberate denial of telemetry (data generated during a missile flight test) about weapon characteristics when that denial would impede verification. But the treaty did not specify which data were needed for verification, so the decision about what telemetry could and could not be encrypted (transmitted in coded form) was left up to the country conducting the tests. In SALT II, the countries also adopted measures that might help them distinguish between the different types of weapons restricted by the treaty; if similar weapons

---

[23] For more information on these arms control regimes, see CRS Report RL33865, *Arms Control and Nonproliferation: A Catalog of Treaties and Agreements*, by Amy F. Woolf, Mary Beth Nikitin, and Paul K. Kerr.

were subject to different limits (such as bombers that could or could not carry nuclear-armed cruise missiles), they had to be built with either "externally observable differences" or, for new types of weapons, "functionally-related observable differences" that could be observed by NTM. SALT II also included the exchange of a simple database listing the numbers of weapons that would be subject to the limits in the treaty.

The arms control agreements signed in the late 1980s and early 1990s built on the provisions that had appeared in earlier treaties. The parties continued to rely on NTM for the bulk of the information needed to monitor restricted forces and activities, but they also expanded the use of cooperative measures that would confirm and add details to the information collected by NTM. The first agreement to include some intrusive cooperative measures, including on-site inspections and aerial overflights, was signed at the Stockholm Conference on Confidence and Security-Building Measures in Europe, in 1986. This agreement, which expanded the Helsinki Accords signed in 1975, included a wide range of measures that were designed to help the countries understand the nature of military operations across Europe. The countries agreed to provide extensive data on military exercises; for some exercises, the countries agreed to invite observers from the other alliance to confirm the information provided in the data exchanges and to confirm that the activity was not threatening to the other alliance.

The 1987 Intermediate-Range Nuclear Forces Treaty (INF) was the first agreement to include an extensive array of cooperative measures that would apply on U.S. and Soviet territory. A number of measures, including the display of ground-launched ballistic missiles on mobile launchers, were designed to deter efforts to deploy ballistic missiles banned by the treaty at bases housing ballistic missiles that were not limited by the treaty. In addition, the countries agreed to exchange detailed data on systems limited by the treaty and to notify the other country when they planned to move or destroy these systems. They also established a continuous monitoring presence outside one INF missile assembly facility in each country. Finally, they agreed to permit on-site inspections at facilities that had housed these systems so that they could confirm the information provided in the data exchanges and collected by NTM.

The 1991 START Treaty followed many of the precedents set by the INF Treaty. It also adopted some measures from the SALT II Treaty, although it added details that addressed some of the uncertainties remaining in that treaty. As with the INF Treaty, START included an extensive data exchange detailing the numbers and locations of affected weapons. START also called for numerous types of on-site inspections, including baseline inspections; inspections of closed-out facilities or eliminated equipment; inspections of "suspect sites" where treaty-limited activities might occur; routine inspections to confirm the accuracy of data provided in the data exchange; and continuous monitoring at assembly facilities for mobile ICBMs. START also allowed the parties to conduct random, short-notice inspections of deployed missiles to confirm that the number of warheads carried on the missiles did not exceed the number listed in the exchanged database.

Under START, the parties were also obligated to provide each other with notifications of several types of activities, such as the movement of items limited by the treaty between declared facilities and the movement of mobile ICBMs when they conducted dispersal exercises. They were also required to display treaty-limited, as well as eliminated, items for a time so that their NTM could gather data on the status of these weapons. Further, in START, the parties agreed that they would not encrypt or otherwise deny access to the telemetry generated during missile flight tests, so that the other side could record this data and use it in evaluating the capabilities of missile systems.

Moreover, they agreed to exchange tapes of this data and other information needed to interpret the data.

Taken together, these provisions allowed each side to draw a comprehensive picture of the other's forces by monitoring and tracking them throughout their service lives. They were counted and measured when they entered the force, monitored while they were deployed, and eliminated according to rigorous rules outlined in the treaty. The level of detail was designed not only to provide comprehensive data, but also to minimize ambiguities and uncertainties that might arise during the treaty's implementation. Although START has expired, the parties retain this data and retain the detailed knowledge it provided them about the other sides' strategic forces. This data will remain valid and useful as long as the two sides continue to deploy and operate the weapons systems that were deployed while START was in force.[24]

The 2002 Strategic Offensive Reductions Treaty (the Moscow Treaty), contained no verification provisions. The Bush Administration argued that this treaty did not need any new monitoring mechanisms because the United States and Russia would continue to use the monitoring mechanisms developed for START. However, even with the information collected by the monitoring mechanisms in START, the United States and Russia did not have the information needed to verify compliance with the Moscow Treaty. To verify compliance, the parties need to be able to understand and identify the difference between permitted and prohibited forces and activities. But the Moscow Treaty contained no agreed definitions that would allow the parties to identify and, therefore, count the warheads limited by the treaty. Each side simply declared the number of warheads it wanted to count under the treaty limits, and neither had the means to confirm the accuracy of this declaration. Moreover, the Moscow Treaty did not restrict the numbers or operations of nuclear forces during the lifetime of the treaty. The parties simply agreed that, on December 31, 2012, they would have no more than 2,200 deployed strategic warheads. Since there were no requirements prior to that time, there was nothing that either party could comply with or violate prior to that time.

Monitoring and Verification in New START

The new START Treaty contains a monitoring and verification regime that resembles the regime in START, in that its text contains detailed definitions of items limited by the treaty; provisions governing the use of NTM to gather data on each side's forces and activities; an extensive database that identifies the numbers, types, and locations of items limited by the treaty; provisions requiring notifications about items limited by the treaty; and inspections allowing the parties to confirm information shared during data exchanges. Because the treaty does not, however, contain limits and restrictions that are identical to those in START, its monitoring and verification regime are not identical to the one in START.

The verification regime in new START also differs from the START regime because the U.S.-Russia relationship has changed and the assumptions about violations and compliance have changed. As noted above, many of the verification provisions in the original START Treaty were designed to detect and deter Soviet efforts to hide or deploy extra missiles and warheads. The

---

[24] Russia has been developing two new missiles that did not count under START. However, since they were tested while START was in force, when Russia had to exchange data on its weapons systems and allow monitoring of its missile tests, the United States has also gathered a significant amount of data on these systems.

United States assumed that the Soviet Union might want to "break out" of the treaty in this way to maintain or gain a strategic advantage over the United States. Some of the verification provisions also sought to reduce the level of uncertainty in the two sides' estimates of each others' forces. For example, because the United States was not certain of the number of mobile missiles that the Soviet Union had produced before START entered into force, it was concerned that some uncounted missiles could be hidden away and left out of the treaty limits.

But times have changed, and the verification regime in new START reflects these changes. The United States would still want to detect and deter Russian efforts to deploy extra missiles and warheads under new START. However, the United States now has a much greater understanding of the number of missiles that Russia has in its stockpile than it did in the late 1980s. It has counted and monitored these missiles for 15 years. It is now far less concerned about the possibility that Russia has hidden extra missiles away in undeclared or unknown facilities. Even if it had done so before START entered into force, these missiles would now be aging and probably lacking appropriate maintenance. Further, the United States may now be less concerned about Russia's incentives to violate the treaty. As Secretary Rumsfeld said of the 2002 Moscow Treaty, Russia had little incentive to exceed the treaty's limits because it planned to reduce its forces to the treaty levels with or without an agreement. The same can be said for Russia in 2010. Most analysts agree that Russia will reduce its forces in coming years, as aging systems retire, with or without an arms control treaty in place.[25]

As a result, the verification regime in the new START Treaty has been streamlined, to make it less costly and complex than the regime in START, and adjusted to reflect the limits in new START and the current circumstances in the relationship between the United States in Russia. In particular, it focuses as much on maintaining transparency, cooperation, and openness as it does on deterring and detecting potential violations.

The discussion that follows reviews some of the limits and restrictions and some of the monitoring and verification provisions in START, and compares them with provisions in new START, to highlight both similarities and differences between the two treaties.[26]

National Technical Means of Verification (NTM)

The provisions governing the use of NTM are in Article IX of START and Article X of new START. They are virtually identical. Both treaties state that "for the purpose of ensuring verification of compliance with the provisions of this Treaty, each Party shall use national technical means of verification at its disposal in a manner consistent with generally recognized principles of international law." Both also indicate that the parties undertake "not to interfere with the national technical means of verification of the other Party" and "not to use concealment measures that impede verification, by national technical means of verification, of compliance with the provisions of this Treaty."

Both treaties also state that

---

[25] http://russianforces.org/blog/2009/01/long-term_force_projections.shtml.

[26] For more details on the monitoring and verification provisions in New START, see CRS Report R41219, *The New START Treaty: Central Limits and Key Provisions*, by Amy F. Woolf.

the obligation not to use concealment measures includes the obligation not to use them at test ranges, including measures that result in the concealment of ICBMs, SLBMs, mobile launchers of ICBMs, or the association between ICBMs or SLBMs and their launchers during testing. The obligation not to use concealment measures shall not apply to cover or concealment practices at ICBM bases and deployment areas, or to the use of environmental shelters for strategic offensive arms.

Hence, even though START and new START both call for extensive data exchanges, cooperation, and on-site inspections to help monitor forces and activities and verify compliance with the agreements, both rely on NTM as the foundation of their verification regimes.

Providing Telemetry Generated During Missile Flight Tests

Telemetry Exchange in START

Among the data collected by NTM are the transmissions broadcast during missile flight tests. These transmissions, known as telemetry, provide information about, among other things, the launch weight and throwweight of the missile,[27] the length of time during which the fuel burned and the missile accelerated, and the number of times the missile maneuvered to release reentry vehicles, that, during an operational launch, would contain a nuclear warhead. In the START Treaty, the United States and Soviet Union agreed that they would not encrypt or otherwise deny access to the telemetry generated during almost all their missile flight tests, so that the other side could record this data and use it in evaluating the capabilities of missile systems. Specifically, Article X of the treaty states, "During each flight test of an ICBM or SLBM, the Party conducting the flight test shall make on-board technical measurements and shall broadcast all telemetric information obtained from such measurements." The activities that are banned because they would deny full access to telemetric information include "the use of encryption, the use of jamming, broadcasting telemetric information from an ICBM or SLBM using narrow directional beaming; and encapsulation of telemetric information, including the use of ejectable capsules or recoverable reentry vehicles."[28]

Moreover, the United States and Soviet Union agreed that they would exchange tapes of this data and other information needed to interpret the data. START did allow exceptions to this ban for missiles that were not capable of recording and broadcasting data and for those that were not covered by the treaty. However, the countries agreed that these exceptions were limited so that it would be difficult to use them to conceal efforts to test new types of ballistic missiles or improved capabilities for existing types of ballistic missiles.

According to the Article-by-Article Legal Analysis that the Bush Administration released with the START Treaty, "access to telemetric information provides useful information about the capability of missiles being tested that assists in verification of Treaty provisions concerning, for example, throw-weight and the number of reentry vehicles."[29] Specifically, information gathered during missile flight tests would help the United States verify Soviet compliance the treaty's limits on

---

[27] Throwweight is the combined weight of the post-boost vehicle, warheads, guidance system, penetration aids, and other equipment found on the front end of a missile. It is considered to be a measure of a missile's destructive capacity because larger missiles with greater throwweight can carry larger or greater numbers of warheads.

[28] http://www.state.gov/documents/organization/27360.pdf.

[29] http://www.state.gov/t/vci/trty/104056 htm#1.

ballistic missile throwweight. Monitoring the number of times the missile simulated or actually released mock warheads would help the United States determine the maximum number of warheads the missile might be equipped to carry. This information would help determine the number of warheads attributed to each type of missile so that the parties could calculate the number of warheads counting against the treaty limits.

Most analysts agree that by monitoring missile flight tests and analyzing telemetric data, both parties to the treaty also acquired a better understanding of the capabilities of the other side's missiles. This transparency may have eased suspicions and avoided "worst-case" assessments about weapons capabilities.

Telemetry Exchange in New START

During the negotiations on the new START Treaty, Russia strongly resisted provisions that would require the broadcast and exchange of telemetry from missile flight tests. It argued that this provision was unfair and created unequal obligations because it was developing new types of missiles and, therefore, broadcasting new data while the United States was only conducting occasional tests of older missiles.

According to press reports, the United States insisted, throughout the negotiations, that the new treaty allow for some broadcast and exchange of telemetry, even though, according to some sources, "new verification and tracking technologies, most of them classified, can provide the same capability without Russians directly providing the data."[30] However, the U.S. intelligence community found telemetry data exchange useful under the old treaty,[31] and according to Ellen Tauscher, the Under Secretary of State for Arms Control and International Security, the "expectation has always been" that telemetry would be included in the new treaty as part of confidence building.[32]

According to press reports, the United States and Russia began to resolve this issue in January 2010, when General Jones, the President's National Security Adviser, and Admiral Mullen, the Chairman of the Joint Chiefs of Staff, went to Moscow. The United States apparently agreed that the new verification regime would not contain a blanket prohibition on telemetry encryption, while Russia agreed that it would exchange telemetry from a small number of missile flight tests each year. As a result, the Protocol to new START indicates that "the Parties shall exchange telemetric information on an equal number of launches of ICBMs and SLBMs, but on no more than five launches of ICBMs and SLBMs each calendar year."[33]

Secretary of Defense Gates noted during the press conference announcing the new treaty "that the United States does not need telemetry from Russian missile flight tests to verify Russian compliance with the treaty."[34] This is because the new treaty does not limit missile throwweight,

---

[30] Josh Rogin, "Rocket Data Dispute Still Unresolved in U.S.-Russia Nuke Talks," *Foreign Policy, The Cable*, January 12, 2010.

[31] Elaine M. Grossman, "New START Pact to Include Missile-Test Transparency, Russian Envoy Says," *Global Security Newswire*, February 18, 2010.

[32] Josh Rogin, "Rocket Data Dispute Still Unresolved in U.S.-Russia Nuke Talks," *Foreign Policy, The Cable*, January 12, 2010.

[33] http://www.state.gov/documents/organization/140047.pdf.

[34] http://www.whitehouse.gov/the-press-office/briefing-secretary-clinton-secretary-gates-admiral-mullen-
(continued...)

and it will not use the maximum number of warheads tested on a missile as the source for the number of warheads assigned to each missile. Nevertheless, the parties agreed to broadcast and exchange some telemetry to increase transparency and ensure a degree of understanding of their strategic offensive forces.

Mobile ICBMs

Limits on Mobile ICBMs in START

The START Treaty limited the United States and the Soviet Union/Russia to 1,100 warheads on mobile ICBMs. These missiles became an issue in the negotiations in the mid-1980s as the Soviet Union began to deploy a single warhead road-mobile ICBM, the SS-25, and a 10-warhead rail-mobile ICBM, the SS-24.[35] Specifically, some analysts questioned whether the United States would be able to monitor Soviet mobile ICBM deployments well enough to count the missiles and verify Soviet compliance with the limits in START. Some also argued that the Soviet Union might be able to stockpile hidden missiles and launchers, and to reload mobile ICBM launchers during a conflict (because the United States could not target and destroy them).

The United States never deployed mobile ICBMs, even though it considered mobile basing for the Peacekeeper missile and, at the time of the START negotiations, was developing a new, small, single-warhead missile that could be deployed on a mobile launcher. Nevertheless, as part of its effort to convince the Soviet Union to accept continuous monitoring at mobile ICBM final assembly facilities, the United States designated the Peacekeeper missile as a mobile type and designated a "final assembly area" at the production facility for the first stage of this missile, so that a U.S. facility would also be subject to perimeter and portal monitoring.

Concerns about the Soviet Union's ability to break out of the treaty limits with mobile ICBMs served as the foundation for the monitoring regime for mobile ICBMs in START. This regime was designed not only to provide the parties with the means to count deployed missiles, but also to limit the ability of either side to "hide" extra missiles near the deployed force or to increase the number of deployed missiles quickly. For example, START limited the numbers of *non-deployed* missiles and *non-deployed* launchers for mobile ICBMs. Each side could retain 250 missiles and 110 launchers for mobile ICBMs, with no more than 125 missiles and 18 launchers for rail mobile ICBMs. This did not eliminate the risk of "breakout," which refers to the rapid addition of stored missiles to the deployed force, but it did limit the magnitude of the breakout potential and the number of missiles that the Soviet Union could "reload" on deployed launchers during a conflict.

To help the parties count these missiles, and to deter efforts to exceed these limits, START contained a number of complementary, and sometimes overlapping, monitoring mechanisms that affected the missiles throughout their service lives. First, START permitted continuous monitoring at missile final assembly facilities so that the parties could count the missiles as they

---

announcement-new-start-tr.

[35] In 1987, the United States began to develop its own mobile ICBM, the 10-warhead MX (Peacekeeper) missile and it continued to explore mobile basing for the new single warhead small ICBM. Although it eventually deployed the Peacekeeper missile in fixed silos, the parties considered it to be a mobile ICBM under the terms of START.

---

entered the force.[36] Prior to START, the United States had used NTM to monitor Soviet ballistic missile production facilities and to estimate the number of ballistic missiles added to the Soviet force. These estimates contained some uncertainty because NTM could not provide information about the activities around the facilities at all times, and because the pace of activity at the facilities made it difficult for NTM to distinguish between vehicles that carried missiles limited by the treaty and those that did not. The perimeter and portal monitoring systems permitted an accurate count of the number of ballistic missiles leaving the facilities and, therefore, a more accurate estimate of the total number of mobile ICBMs in the Soviet force.

The parties also agreed to record the serial numbers, referred to in the treaty as "unique identifiers," for the mobile ICBMs, both for those in existence when the treaty entered into force and on new missiles as they left the production facilities. These numbers were listed in the agreed database and were used to help track and identify permitted missiles.[37] The parties could check the serial numbers during on-site inspections to confirm that the missiles they encountered were those that they expected to see at the facility during the inspection. This would complicate Soviet efforts to bring extra missiles into declared facilities, either for deployment or maintenance, because they might be discovered during a short-notice, random inspection.

START mandated that the parties provide notifications when mobile ICBMs moved between permitted facilities. These included "notification, no less than 24 hours in advance, of the departure of each deployed mobile launcher of ICBMs and its associated missile from a restricted area, rail garrison, or other facility, for a relocation" and "notification, no later than 48 hours after the arrival of each deployed mobile launcher of ICBMs and its associated missile at its destination" These notifications not only allowed each party to keep track of the mobile ICBMs, but also complicated evasion efforts such as moving known missiles out of the force and into hidden locations or moving hidden missiles into the deployed force.

START also mandated that the parties provide notifications when mobile ICBMs moved out of their main operating bases for an exercise. They had to provide notification "no later than 18 hours after the beginning of an exercise dispersal" and notification, "no later than eight hours after the completion of an exercise dispersal." In addition, each party had the right to conduct "post-dispersal inspections of deployed mobile launchers of ICBMs and their associated missiles" to determine, using the unique identifiers, whether the missiles returning from the exercise were missiles that were supposed to be deployed at that base.

Finally, missiles and launchers removed from the force had to be eliminated according to specific procedures outlined in the treaty. This not only helped the parties keep an accurate count of the deployed missiles, but served as a further deterrent to efforts to hide extra missiles outside the treaty regime.

Taken together, these provisions provided something of a "cradle-to-grave" monitoring regime for mobile ICBMs. While this regime would not have prevented a determined Soviet effort to produce and hide some number of extra mobile ICBMs, it was designed to complicate such an

---

[36] The perimeter/portal continuous monitoring systems (PPCMS) consisted of fences surrounding the entire perimeter of the facility and one restricted portal through which all vehicles large enough to carry items limited by the treaty (such as the first stage of a mobile ICBM) had to pass. The portal contained scales and other measuring devices that the countries could use to determine whether the vehicle carried an item limited by the treaty.

[37] Article IX, paragraph 4 of START states that "to aid verification, each ICBM for mobile launchers of ICBMs shall have a unique identifier as provided for in the Inspection Protocol."

effort and raise the risk of detection if the Soviet Union ever tried to mix hidden missiles in with the deployed force.

Mobile ICBMs in New START

The new START Treaty does not contain a sublimit on mobile ICBMs or their warheads. It also does not contain any limits on the number of non-deployed mobile ICBMs or the number of non-deployed mobile ICBM launchers. These launchers and warheads will, however, count under the aggregate limits set by the treaty. As a result, the United States will still need to count or estimate the number of mobile ICBMs in Russia's force. As was true with START, the United States would need this number not only to verify compliance with the treaty limits, but also to deter Russian efforts to break out of the limits with hidden missiles and launchers.

However, the task of monitoring mobile ICBMs may be less complicated in the current environment. After 15 years of START implementation, the United States has far less uncertainty in its estimate of the number of mobile ICBMs in Russia's strategic forces. Moreover, Russia is producing new missiles at a far lower rate than the Soviet Union produced them during the 1980s, so the United States may find it easier to keep track of missile production with NTM.

New START will not permit perimeter and portal monitoring at missile assembly facilities. Russia withdrew its presence from the United States years ago, when the United States stopped producing motors for the Peacekeeper missiles.[38] The United States shut down its operations at Votkinsk, where Russia produced the SS-25 missile and now produces the SS-27 and RS-24 missiles, in early December,\ 2009, as START was about to expire.[39] The parties must, however, provide notification at least 48 hours before the time when all items limited by the treaty, including mobile ICBMs, leave production facilities.

They parties will not, however, have to provide notifications when mobile ICBMs begin or conclude an exercise dispersal. They also will not be permitted to conduct "post-dispersal" inspections, although they will be able to conduct on-site inspections at mobile ICBM deployment areas as part of the routine inspection process.

The parties will continue to list the serial numbers, or unique identifiers, for mobile ICBMs in the shared database. Moreover, in contrast with START, they will record these numbers for all ICBMs, SLBMs, and heavy bombers covered by the limits in the new treaty, and will use them to verify the location of all treaty-limited items during on-site inspections. When items limited by the treaty, including mobile ICBMs, move from one facility to another, the parties will have to update the database so each facility contains a complete list of each item and its unique identifier located at that facility. Then, according to the Protocol to the treaty, "inspectors shall have the right to read the unique identifiers on all designated deployed ICBMs or designated deployed SLBMs, non-deployed ICBMs, non-deployed SLBMs, and designated heavy bombers that are located at the inspection site."[40] Hence, as was true in START, the parties will have the opportunity to confirm that items located at the facilities are supposed to be there. As was true

---

[38] Elaine M. Grossman, "U.S. Treaty-Monitoring Presence at Russian Missile Plant Winding Down," *Global Security Newswire*, November 20, 2009.

[39] Nicholas Kralev, "U.S. to Stop Counting New Missiles in Russia," *Washington Times*, December 1, 2009, p. 1.

[40] http://www.state.gov/documents/organization/140047.pdf.

under START, this provision may deter efforts to mix uncounted systems in with deployed systems, as they might be identified during an inspection.

Some have suggested that several characteristics of new START will complicate the United States' ability to obtain enough information to monitor with confidence the number of mobile ICBMs in Russia's missile force. For example, the treaty will not allow an independent count of the number of new missiles entering the force. In addition, some argue that because Russia will provide the list of serial numbers for its missiles, the United States will not be able to confirm that each missile's serial number is truly a unique number. Moreover, because the United States will not receive notifications before and after exercise dispersals, and because it will not be able to inspect deployment areas after these exercises, Russia might be able to bring extra missiles into the deployment areas when returning from an exercise.

U.S. negotiators have insisted that, despite the factors listed above, the United States will still have "cradle-to-grave" monitoring for mobile ICBMs. Even though U.S. inspectors will not record the serial numbers themselves, they will be able to confirm those numbers during on-site inspections. And, in the current environment, there is less chance that Russia would be able to hide away extra missiles because the production rates at its ICBM facilities are so low. During the 1980s, the Soviet Union produced dozens of new missiles each year; Russia now adds, on average, only six to seven missile per year to its force.[41] As Under Secretary of State Ellen Tauscher said when asked about the U.S. ability to monitor Russia's mobile ICBMs without monitoring at the Votkinsk facility, "we have a very good history from the START regime as far as verification and confidence ... [we] do not have the same kind of oversight over Votinsk as we did in the original START treaty. But at the same time, we believe that we have enough enhanced transparency and supplemental verification that will give us everything that we need."[42]

On-Site Inspections

On-Site Inspections in START

The 1991 START Treaty contained 12 different types of on-site inspections. These are summarized on **Table 1**, below. These inspections did not serve as an independent source of information; they were intended to provide the parties with the means to confirm information collected by NTM or shared in data exchanges and notifications. Nevertheless, as participants in the inspection process have noted, the parties did gather useful information about the weapons systems, facilities, and procedures that was not directly related to the limits in the treaty. Moreover, the inspections fostered a level of communication and cooperation that helped to ease suspicions and reduce the possibility of misunderstandings. Hence, although they were designed with the narrow role of confirming information, they ended up playing a much broader role in ensuring transparency and predictability.

Several of the START inspections confirmed baseline information that could help in later efforts to monitor compliance. These included inspections designed to confirm the technical

---

[41] According to one U.S. inspector, monitoring at Votkinsk "was very monotonous. We could have months go by without inspecting a missile." See Elaine M. Grossman, "U.S. Treaty-Monitoring Pressence at Russian Missile Plant Winding Down," *Global Security Newswire*, November 20, 2009.

[42] http://www.state.gov/t/us/139205 htm.

characteristics of missiles, launchers, and bombers limited by the treaty; inspections designed to distinguish between bombers that could and could not carry cruise missiles; and inspections designed to distinguish between bombers that could and could not carry nuclear weapons. Although the parties could monitor some of these characteristics with NTM, and received further details in mandated data exchanges, the added transparency afforded by these inspections helped increase confidence in and understanding of the weapons deployed by each side. New weapons added after the treaty entered into force were subject to similar data exchanges and inspections.

Table 1. On-Site Inspections in START

Type of inspection	Timing/Frequency	Rationale
Baseline	Between 45 and 165 days after entry into force of the treaty. One inspection at each declared facility.	To confirm the accuracy of data on the numbers and types of items specified for such facilities in the initial exchange of data.
New facility	Beginning 45 days after entry into force; inspection must occur within 60 days of notification of new facility.	To confirm the accuracy of data on the numbers and types of items specified in the notifications of new facilities.
Data Update and Suspect Site	Beginning 165 days after entry into force. Combined quota of 15 data update and suspect site inspections each year, with a maximum of two per year at any one facility.	To confirm the accuracy of data on the numbers and types of items specified for such facilities in the notifications and regular exchanges of updated data.
Re-entry vehicle inspections	Beginning 165 days after entry into force. Annual quota of 10 reentry vehicle inspections, with a maximum of two per year at any one base.	To confirm that such ballistic missiles contain no more reentry vehicles than the number of warheads attributed to them.
Formerly declared facility	Beginning 165 days after entry into force. Annual quota of three formerly declared facility inspections each year, with no more than two per year at any one facility.	To confirm that facilities that have been notified as eliminated are not being used for purposes inconsistent with this treaty.
Post-exercise dispersal inspections of deployed mobile launchers of ICBMs and their associated missiles	Number of inspections depends on number of exercise dispersals.	To confirm that the number of mobile launchers of ICBMs and their associated missiles located at the base does not exceed the number specified for that ICBM base.
Conversion and elimination	Beginning 45 days after entry into force, as needed after completion of the conversion or elimination process.	To confirm the conversion or elimination of strategic offensive arms (as specified in the Conversion or Elimination Protocol).
Closeout	Within 60 days after notification of the elimination of the facility.	To confirm that the elimination of facilities has been completed.
Inspection during technical characteristics exhibitions	Exhibitions of existing systems are to be completed no later than 45 days after entry into force of the treaty.	To permit the inspecting Party to confirm that technical characteristics correspond to the data specified for these items.

Type of inspection	Timing/Frequency	Rationale
Distinguishability Inspections for heavy bombers, former heavy bombers, and long-range nuclear ALCMs	Exhibitions of existing systems are to be completed no later than 45 days after entry into force of the treaty.	To confirm that the technical characteristics of each type and each variant of such heavy bombers correspond to the data specified for that bomber; to demonstrate that bombers and former heavy bombers are distinguishable from each other and from each variant of heavy bombers of the same type equipped for long-range nuclear ALCMs; to confirm that the technical characteristics of each type and each variant of such long-range ALCMs correspond to the data specified for these items; to demonstrate differences, that make long-range non-nuclear ALCMs distinguishable from long-range nuclear ALCMs.
Baseline inspections during exhibitions of heavy bombers equipped for non-nuclear armaments, all training heavy bombers, and all former heavy bombers	Conducted during the period for baseline inspections.	To demonstrate that such airplanes satisfy the requirements for conversion in accordance with the Conversion or Elimination Protocol.

Source: U.S. Department of State, Article-by-Article Analysis of START Treaty, http://www.state.gov/t/vci/trty/104058.htm#5.

Some of the START inspections were designed to confirm that weapons or facilities removed from the treaty database were truly incapable of performing strategic missions. For example, closeout and former facility inspections were intended to confirm that facilities once used to support or house weapons limited by the treaty were no longer performing that mission, after one party informed the other of that change. Elimination and conversion inspections served the same purpose for weapons; after one party completed the process outlined in the treaty to eliminate or convert weapons so that they could be removed from accountability, the other party had the right to inspect the eliminated weapons and confirm that the process was complete. The rules governing these close-outs, eliminations, and conversions, when combined with the inspections confirming their completion, also deterred violations by making it difficult for either side to operate facilities secretly or to retain weapons that no longer counted under the treaty limits.

Some of the START inspections were designed to provide the parties with the opportunity to confirm data on the numbers and locations of weapons limited by the treaty. These include the baseline inspections that occurred at declared facilities within the first few months after the treaty entered into force and new facility inspections that served the same purpose for facilities that started to house treaty-limited weapons in the years after the treaty entered into force; data update and suspect site inspections that occurred annually while the treaty remained in force; and post-exercise dispersal inspections that occurred after mobile ICBMs returned from a dispersal exercise. Every facility that housed treaty limited items was subject to a baseline inspection. All the declared facilities and a small number of "suspect sites" that were listed in the treaty's database were also subject to up to 15 short-notice inspections to confirm the data on the numbers and types of weapons at that facility. Each mobile ICBM deployment area could also be inspected after each exercise.

These inspections were not intended to provide the baseline information about the total number of weapons or even the numbers of weapons at each facility; that information came from NTM and data exchanges. They were, however, designed to deter and detect violations by making it more difficult to mix hidden weapons systems in with declared, deployed forces at the bases and facilities that were designed to support these weapons. The Soviet Union might still have tried to deploy extra missiles at undeclared or hidden facilities, but this scenario was thought to be more costly and more risky since evidence of the presence of any treaty-limited items outside of declared facilities would raise questions about a possible treaty violation.

START also permitted each side to conduct up to 10 random, short-notice reentry vehicle inspections each year to confirm that the number of warheads deployed on a type of missile did not exceed the number attributed to that type of missile in the shared database. These inspections were not used to *establish* how many reentry vehicles could be carried on a particular type of ballistic missile or to *count* the total number of deployed warheads. They were intended to deter efforts to add extra warheads to the missiles. The party hosting the inspection would not know which missile the inspectors would select and the short notice preceding an inspection would make it extremely difficult to remove extra warheads and conceal evidence of a violation. Since the parties could shield the front end of the missile during the inspection, as long as the maximum number of reentry vehicles was evident, the inspections would not reveal the structure or electronics of the missile's front end. As a result, the inspections did not necessarily reveal the actual number of warheads on a missile if that number fell below the number listed in the database, but they could confirm that the number did not exceed the number in the database.

On-Site Inspections in New START

The verification regime in new START will include on-site inspections and exhibitions as part of a comprehensive monitoring and verification regime.[43] At the same time, Administration officials have stated that this regime will be simpler, less costly, and more streamlined than the inspection regime in START. Specifically, the regime will include fewer numbers and fewer types of on-site inspections than the old START Treaty, but the parties will be able achieve several inspection goals during a single inspections.

The parties will not conduct baseline inspections or exhibitions to confirm the number of weapons housed at each facility or to confirm the technical characteristics of those weapons. The baseline information for the new START Treaty is the same as the concluding information from the old START Treaty. This data was updated in July 2009 and is unlikely to have changed much since then. As was noted above, the United States also will not be able to conduct post-dispersal inspections after mobile ICBM exercise dispersals.

At the same time, new START does allow exhibitions so that the parties can "demonstrate distinguishing features and confirm technical characteristics of new types of weapons." They can also use exhibitions "to demonstrate the results" when a weapon limited by the treaty is converted into a weapon that is no longer limited by the treaty. Moreover, both parties will be able to conduct random, short-notice inspections at all the facilities listed in the treaty that can house deployed and non-deployed systems. These inspections are scheduled to begin 60 days after New START enters into force, so they will begin in early April 2011. New START divides these inspections into two categories: Type One inspections and Type Two inspections. It further states that each side can conduct up to 10 Type One inspections and up to eight Type Two inspections.

---

[43] The White House, Office of the Press Secretary, *Key Facts About the New START Treaty*, Washington, D.C., March 26, 2010, http://www.whitehouse.gov/the-press-office/key-facts-about-new-start-treaty.

Type One Inspections

Type One inspections are those that will occur at ICBM bases, submarine bases, and air bases that house deployed or non-deployed launchers, missiles, and bombers. They will use these inspections "to confirm the accuracy of declared data on the numbers and types of deployed and non-deployed strategic offensive arms subject to this Treaty. During Type One inspections, the parties will also be able to confirm that the number of warheads located on deployed ICBMs and deployed SLBMs; and the number of nuclear armaments located on deployed heavy bombers" are consistent with the numbers listed in the treaty database. Under START, these two types of inspections had to occur at different times and counted against two inspection quotas. Under new START, they can occur at the same time and only count as one inspection against the treaty quota.

The reentry vehicle inspections in new START will also be distinctly different from the inspections in START because the counting rules for ballistic missiles have changed. Under START, the treaty database listed the number of warheads *attributed* to a type of missile, and each missile of that type counted as the same number of warheads. The parties then inspected the missiles to confirm that the number of warheads on a particular missile did not exceed the number attributed to that type of missile. The database in new START will list the number of warheads actually *deployed* on each individual missile. It will not count each missile in a given type as if all missiles of that type carry the same number of warheads. And the total number of warheads counted against ICBMs and SLBMs will be equal to the actual number of warheads deployed on those missiles. During Type One inspections, the parties will have the right to designate one ICBM or one SLBM for inspection, and when inspecting that missile, the parties will be able to count the actual number of warheads deployed on the missile. The inspected party can still cover the reentry vehicles to protect information not related to the number of warheads, but the party must use individual covers for each reentry vehicle, so that the actual number of warheads on the missile is evident to the inspectors.

As was true in START, the parties will not use these inspections to calculate the total number of warheads carried on deployed missiles. Ten inspections each year will not provide that kind of information. But because the inspections will be random, and will occur on short notice, they have some chance of detecting an effort by the other party to deploy a missile with more than its declared number of warheads. Therefore, the inspections may deter efforts to conceal extra warheads on the deployed force. And as is the intent in new START, inspections that allow the parties to count the actual number of deployed warheads may lead provide a degree of transparency and understanding that would not be available without the monitoring regime in new START.

Type Two Inspections

Under new START, the parties will conduct Type Two inspections at facilities that house non-deployed or converted launchers and missiles. These include "ICBM loading facilities; SLBM loading facilities; storage facilities for ICBMs, SLBMs, and mobile launchers of ICBMs; repair facilities for ICBMs, SLBMs, and mobile launchers of ICBMs; test ranges; and training facilities." They will use these inspections "to confirm the accuracy of declared technical characteristics and declared data, specified for such facilities, on the number and types of non-deployed ICBMs and non-deployed SLBMs, first stages of ICBMs and SLBMs, and non-deployed launchers of ICBMs." In addition, they can conduct these inspections at formerly declared facilities, "to confirm that such facilities are not being used for purposes inconsistent with this Treaty." They will also use Type Two inspections to confirm that solid-fueled ICBMs, solid-fueled SLBMs, or mobile launchers of ICBMs have been eliminated according to treaty procedures.

With the two different types of inspections, the United States and Russia will each be able to conduct 18 random, short-notice inspections each year. However, because the Type One inspections can achieve two goals during one inspection, this is essentially equivalent to the 28 random, short-notice inspections permitted under START (10 reentry vehicle on-site inspections, 15 data update and suspect site inspections, and 3 former declared facility inspections). Moreover, Russia had 60 facilities that were subject to inspection. Now, under new START, it may have only 34 facilities. Hence, according to U.S. officials, the United States will conduct inspections at a greater proportion of Russia's facilities.

Exhibitions

According to the Protocol to new START, "exhibitions shall be conducted at the invitation of the Party conducting the exhibition, separately from inspections, at the locations and in the periods of time chosen by the Party conducting the exhibition."[44] The treaty does not require that the parties conduct or participate in exhibitions, but it does indicate that these would provide an opportunity for the parties "to demonstrate the distinguishing features and to confirm technical characteristics of each new type, variant, or version of an ICBM, SLBM, heavy bomber equipped for nuclear armaments." They can also use the exhibitions "to demonstrate the results of the conversion of the first item of a type of ICBM launcher, SLBM launcher, or heavy bomber equipped for nuclear armaments" when the conversion is designed to remove the type of launcher or heavy bomber from accountability under the treaty.

The parties will list the distinguishing features and technical characteristics of new types of missiles and bombers in the treaty database. The exhibitions will add transparency to that process, by giving the parties the opportunity to view and understand the differences between weapons systems, particularly for those that have been converted to other uses. This information may be helpful in deterring or detecting violations of the treaty. It also encourages transparency and openness, and may increase understanding of the capabilities of weapons limited by the treaty.

Assessing the Verification Regime in New START

Participants in the debate about the new START Treaty, both in the Senate and in the public at large, sought to compare the verification regimes in the two treaties to determine whether the regime in the new START Treaty can provide the United States with the information it needs to effectively verify Russian compliance. But this comparison could not, by itself, provide useful answers about the verifiability of the new START Treaty if it simply compared the lists of inspections, notifications, data exchanges, and cooperative activities mandated by the two treaties. Even though more transparency and cooperation may be preferred in the abstract, the monitoring measures in the new treaty "should be determined by the treaty's specific limits and the need to verify those limits."[45]

---

[44] http://www.state.gov/documents/organization/140047.pdf.

[45] Steven Pifer and Strobe Talbott, "Judging the new START Treaty," *Politico*, March 29, 2010.

As noted earlier, no verification regime can provide the United States with absolute confidence that Russia will comply with all the limits in the treaty, or absolute assurances that the United States will be able to detect any Russian effort to evade the limits. Even if the United States is confident that it could detect militarily significant violations in time to respond and offset any threats to its security, there will be some risk that noncompliant activity may go undetected for some time. Depending on the weight one places on this risk, the possibility that Russia might pursue undetected violations might be argued as grounds to reject the treaty.

Alternatively, some might conclude that, even with some uncertainties in the verification regime, the treaty serves U.S. interests because the United States would have far less access to and knowledge about Russian forces without any treaty-mandated monitoring provisions in place. The new START Treaty will contain an extensive database, listing the number and location of every deployed and non-deployed delivery vehicle and every deployed and non-deployed missile in the Russian arsenal. The database will also list the precise number of warheads deployed on each missile. This information would be unavailable if the United States and Russia had not signed the new START Treaty. Moreover, the Obama Administration, and others outside government, have concluded that the cooperation and transparency afforded by the new verification regime can serve to ease tensions and foster a better relationship between the United States and Russia. Specifically, some see the verification regime in the new START Treaty as an effort to build "a foundation of trust with Moscow."[46]

The sufficiency of new START's verification regime is just one factor that might be weighed in a broader net assessment of the contribution that the new treaty might make to U.S. national security. Some have argued that the new treaty will do little to strengthen U.S. security because Russia, even in the absence of a treaty, may reduce its aging forces in the coming years, and because Russia no longer poses enough of a threat to U.S. security for the United States to warrant an agreement limiting Moscow's nuclear forces.

Others, however, see the treaty as "tangible evidence of a new partnership between the United States and Russia" and argue that creates momentum "towards a revamped nuclear security regime."[47] They further argue that the new START Treaty, and renewed cooperation between the United States and Russia, can contribute to U.S. nonproliferation goals. Progress on U.S.-Russian arms control may convince other nations that the United States is serious about meeting its obligations under the Nuclear Nonproliferation Treaty (NPT) and may convince more nations to join with the United States in both trying to strengthen the NPT regime and trying to isolate Iran and North Korea in the international community.

These benefits may be difficult to measure and hard to factor into a net assessment of the value of the new START Treaty. Nevertheless, some argue that, when combined with the fact that the treaty will provide the United States with unprecedented access to information about Russian nuclear forces and a measure of predictability about the future direction of those forces, the benefits of the treaty to U.S. national security interests far outweigh any uncertainties that may arise due to the changes in the verification regime.[48]

---

[46] Peter Baker and Helene Cooper, "Obama Completes Arms Control Deal With Russia," *New York Times*, March 25, 2010.

[47] Peter Baker and Helene Cooper, "Obama Completes Arms Control Deal With Russia," *New York Times*, March 25, 2010.

[48] Steven Pifer, *New START: Good News For Arms Control*, Arms Control Association, Washington, D.C., April 2, (continued...)

Author Contact Information

Amy F. Woolf
Specialist in Nuclear Weapons Policy
awoolf@crs.loc.gov, 7-2379

(...continued)
2010, http://www.armscontrol.org/act/2010_05/Pifer.

www.ingramcontent.com/pod-product-compliance
Lightning Source LLC
Chambersburg PA
CBHW081418170526
45166CB00010B/3386